I0799532

"Grant Chemidlin's poems in *In the Middle of a Better World* aren't afraid of authenticity and honesty. They traffic in truth, whether they are the truth of coming out or the truth of love and human connection in a challenging world. Everything is tangled in Chemidlin's poems because the book seems to make a beautiful case for rising out of difficulty, rising in difficulty, and rising before difficulty, as 'Man Marries Man' seems to say: '& when the breeze blows / with the hum of our vows, the strings that kept both / our hidden selves bound will fall beside our feet. There, / we'll stand. There, we'll be.'"

— VICTORIA CHANG
author of *With My Back to the World*

"'Each boy / has no shadow, in the firelight, dancing / untethered.' How gloriously free, this image. How vital, to be this free. And how dangerous, to find such freedom, to continue living, dancing, this way. Formally inventive, full of sensual detail and psychological insight, this book examines homophobia, in particular internalized homophobia, and all the ways out—out of the closet, out of the fear, into joy and sex and tenderness and community and self-knowledge and love. Grant Chemidlin's work makes me grateful all over again for poetry and for queer people."

— CHEN CHEN
author of *Your Emergency Contact Has Experienced an Emergency*

"How often does a poem make you smile? Turn up one corner of your mouth in sweet recognition? Grant Chemidlin's *In the Middle of a Better World* made me feel as though I was seated beside a friend, holding his hand, holding the truth that is compassion, intimacy, grace. These poems explore shame, and the magic of what waits to be discovered—our true selves—on the other side of its shimmering, transformative fire. I felt such queer kinship with these poems, such gratitude for their charming, delicately wrought steps across the page. 'People are impossible to fully know,' writes Chemidlin. 'Starry sky we try to trap / in a thimble.' Turn to these poems when you feel the world has lost its mystery. Be reminded there's still so much—sparkling, winking—just on the other side of what we fear and desire most."

— KEETJE KUIPERS
author of *Lonely Women Make Good Lovers*

"*In the Middle of a Better World* carries us from the fearful, lonely dark of the closet out into the bright, brilliant clarity of the self understood. Grant Chemidlin's better world is enriched by conflict, pain, and resolution, by family and friendship, by earnest sex and ecstatic love. It is an adventure in the quotidian surreal. Here we find the beloved picking up and folding a pool of sunlight from the floor, Jesus flying high overhead in a fighter jet, a twink walking into the Republican National Convention. Here we find a poet discovering himself and sharing his discoveries with unabashed generosity, courage, and joy."

— JASWINDER BOLINA
author of *English as a Second Language and Other Poems*

"A boldly sumptuous collection, Grant Chemidlin's *In the Middle of a Better World* never flinches from either ecstasy or uncertainty found in the erotic and mystical spaces where the body and the natural world touch. In striking poems with surprising turns, speakers wrestle with coming out, go to leather bars, or meet at night in the snow where 'the sweet & the scary' is transformed through presences that deepen the search for belonging both in this world and a better one. Bodies morph into books or trees, mingle with moss and hummingbirds and tongues. Chemidlin's poems reclaim this magic in a world that would deny it, especially during a time of great suffering. Men are hopeful in each other's arms or bond in marriage, yet still they remain in the middle of a better world. But Chemidlin's remarkable collection finds its bliss in the striving itself, and the dare that is to imagine that better world."

— CHRISTIAN GULLETTE
author of *Coachella Elegy*

IN THE MIDDLE OF A BETTER WORLD

POEMS

GRANT CHEMIDLIN

central avenue
2026

Copyright © 2026 Grant Chemidlin
Cover and internal design © 2026 Central Avenue Marketing Ltd.
Cover Illustration: The Donchester – the Cluett Dress Shirt (1911)
by Joseph Christian Leyendecker

All rights reserved. No part of this book may be used or reproduced in any manner whatsoever without written permission from the author except in the case of brief quotations embodied in critical articles and reviews.

This book is a work of creative expression. Although it draws upon the author's personal experiences, it includes fictionalized elements, alterations, and composite characters for literary effect. As such, it should not be read as a literal or factual account. Any resemblance to actual persons, living or dead, or to actual events is purely coincidental or used in a fictionalized manner.

Published by Central Avenue Poetry, an imprint of Central Avenue Marketing Ltd.
centralavenuepublishing.com

IN THE MIDDLE OF A BETTER WORLD: Poems

978-1-77168-436-1 (pbk)
978-1-77168-437-8 (ebk)

Printed in United States of America

1. POETRY / LGBTQ+ 2. POETRY / Subjects & Themes - Love & Erotica

3 5 7 9 10 8 6 4 2

for Brian

Contents

The Beginning of Love 1

I

f a g [irst pet ls in . . .] 5
The Prayers of Mice 6
Pickup Trucks 7
Cruising 8
The Mysterious Missing Story 10
f a g [Ben, best riend . . .] 11
In the Hour of Want 12
Gay Voice 13
The Poker Game 14
Little Quaint House 15
Table Talk 17
Vitruvian Boy 18
Portrait of a Partially Abandoned Campground 20

II

Visitation 25
Leather Bars 26
Amy 27
f a g [Coworker Jim, irst . . .] 29
A Water Cycle 30
Celebrity 31
After Seeing Queer Teens Holding Hands on the Sidewalk 35
Witches 37
At the Protest, I List the Consequences of Coming Out 38
He Came to Me Again Last Night 39
This Halloween 40
Heatwave 41
Tiny Pants 43

III

The News That Fell like Heavy Rain 47
Man Marries Man 49
When the World Ends, We Take Turns Playing Dress-up 50
As the City Burned 51

Still, Days 52
What You Forgot 53
The Garden State 54
On the Phone 56
Rain on the Fourth 57
Closer 58
f a g [Do I count . . .] 60
On the Eve of Our Wedding 61
A Summer Camp Wedding 62
His Finger with the Ninja Turtles Band-Aid 67

IV

First Time We've Seen Her Since the Wedding 71
Too Many Loose Shoes in the Closet 72
Our First Turkey 73
Dinner Party 74
f a g [riendly older wom n . . .] 75
I Hear the Shower Shutting Off 76
Reflex 77
f a g [in lly posted the . . .] 79
The Homosexual Agenda 80
Copyright 84
Airbnb 85
Rain 87
At the End of Another Sad Gay Movie 88
From the Window 89
After Reading My New Manuscript 90
The Future 92
For if I Go First 93

. . .

Dark Sunday 97
Notes 99
Acknowledgments 100
About the Author 102

IN THE MIDDLE OF A BETTER WORLD

THE BEGINNING OF LOVE

As we walked down the dirt path,

he reached up & plucked a small fluff

of cloud from the sky, then popped it

in his mouth like cotton candy.

Want some? he said, pulling another.

How did you do that? I said.

I don't know, he said. *I was just hungry.*

I knew right then the power he would have
over me.

His hands. *His hands.*

I couldn't stop staring.

• • •

I

irst we le rn silence is olden.

First we learn silence is golden.

First we learn silence is golden.

First we learn silence is golden.

First we learn silence is golden.

First we le**a**rn silence is **g**olden.

FAG

irst pet ls in sprin — ield ripe with little mirrors.

Open, they'd s y, *row*, but I e red their

i ted cert inty. To keep doubt bloomin ,

or me, me nt immunity, od, my ther, this

blessed country.

THE PRAYERS OF MICE

You make friends with the three palm trees standing tall
outside your window, make two peanut butter & jelly sandwiches
& save the one for later, for dinner maybe, whereafter,
you'll do the dishes & hum a sad song about love,
about what goes wrong, so when the time finally comes,
you'll feel you're ready. Before bed, you suddenly wonder
what the fox-trot is, so you google it, practice all its steps
in leather boots, which drives the mouse living in your walls
to bang a Q-tip paw against the wood. Even he
(the fear-driven mouse) feels sorry for you,
goes to sleep each night praying that tomorrow
brings you courage.

PICKUP TRUCKS

This town is full of them,
almost as many as there are trees—coniferous & tall
as the oldest stories.
When I see one I feel immediate unease
like I've crossed a boundary
where I don't belong.
The red one. White with black stripe.
Tires bigger than the circus wheels
they strapped women to
then threw knives.
Useful—for hard jobs & heavy loads,
the grit & dirt of building your own, of which
I know nothing.
& yet, at least to me, still
a symbol—a grill bent
into a scowl, headlights howling out
into the night, as if to say *Look,*
look into these eyes.
I dare you.

CRUISING

Two men meet in the middle
of a secret,

hide behind
the bushes. The trees,

who see no deviance, offer
their trunks for cover.

Two men meet in the middle
of desire, slip out

of their armor, bask
in the unclad sun,

in each other's arms,
in each other's tongues.

In the middle
of a better world:

Two men, undone.
Two men, unbelievably soft

when they touch. Even
the stubble-studded chins

are silken moss.
A twig-crack. A gruff shout

in the distance
& two men

disappear.
All that's left—two hollowed logs

holding their breath

on the forest floor.

THE MYSTERIOUS MISSING STORY

I'm an open book, he says.

I think more bookshelf, she says,

grabbing hold of a thin section of his abdomen

& pulling out a leather-bound book.

She leafs through it, then slides it back, laughs,

I've read that one.

He laughs too & turns to pour the coffee.

Her shifting eye catching the empty slot

in his right shoulder.

F A G

Ben, best riend, s ys rushin   is cool.

  r ternities like Phi Si   will turn us

into men.   irm knock. Ben, chosen, w lks

out the dorm. The bunk beds   row   ive stories,

or just one. I tell it over & over to my sh dow

I tuck into Ben's bed below. But the story's end

is wron . Their silence, my   ilure,

loosened the   lued word   rom my

mouth—b t clutched upside down. No,

the son bird.

IN THE HOUR OF WANT

When the night-wind pushes open the window,
you think it's his fingers on your skin.
Then, once again—the wings,
up & out they tear from your back
like weeds, two half-moons, tattered, iridescent
feathers. They wake you. They pull you
from the sheets. You grab
the bedpost. You grab
the dresser's knob, feet dangling. You fight
like honest gravity. You say, Stop. *Stop*. He doesn't want
to see us
anymore.

GAY VOICE

Little moon, little hilltop
of the throat, little bloom—
orchids petalled white,
night-breeze like a silk dress.
The queen peacock is fast
asleep. Holes
in the grass where crickets
should be, but there are fireflies,
star-flecks, a red, teeming
planet. Keep it far. Keep it
quiet. Keep mouth closed
so the sun never rises. Light,
with its violent
hands, can do so much
damage—
like growth, the freedom
to roam, the pink sheep
finally able to graze,
the queen peacock
awake, ready to rule.

THE POKER GAME

We all look the same, ~~cute~~ suits, smoke,
poised men with clean shaves. They don't realize
I'm bluffing. I
don't realize I'm bluffing, but when I do
the cigar I'm holding *poofs*
into a penis, another man's
penis, my lips, now leeches. The other men see it,
faces corkscrew
in disgust. Worse
than scream,
they laugh. *But my hat,* I point. *My loose, pin-striped*
pants!
The penis sprouts a naked man.
Thank god, I say. *Another faggot.*
He steps back,
I'm not gay if you're blowing me.
The room nods. The naked man grabs a chair,
sits.
But this is my poem, I say.
No, the men say. *It's not. It never was, you just*
wanted it to be.
I look up—
the wall, once
a bruise, now
a cute blue door.

LITTLE QUAINT HOUSE

outside, but stepping in, the walls were adorned
with naked men. Stretched, voluptuous, leather-bound
& gagged, tasteful, but for my still-
closeted eyes—the silver glint of the sharpest needle.

I looked both ways before crossing
the hall—past the marble ass, *Tom of Finland* quiet
on the table. It was like finding
a library buried in sand, contraband of a bunker,
the kind of bachelor's pad I'd never even thought
to dream of.

He was the only out man I knew,
so I invited myself over.
We drank gin, kissed
on the couch, my first time feeling the coarse ground
of a man's face against my own.

The friction. The heat
of his unbuttoning, of him leading me up the spiral stairs
to the bedroom.
Both bare, I saw our cocks
were nearly identical—in size, in straightness, only his had aged
twenty years. The image

scared me. I became suddenly aware
of something cavernous, a sadness

that tinged the room, pooled among shadows, the faces
of the men trapped in black frames.

I was young, so did that awful thing—
we came, at the same time, then I
left him. Drove home, back
to what, for me, was just
beginning.

TABLE TALK

Mom, I'm

Look, the sky, isn't it so

I've been

The trash, please take it out after

Do I need to say

Your father

Our Father, Who art in

Pass the salt and

I'm trying to

Leave the dishes on

My chest, this heavy

Chocolate or French

Why won't you

Listen, I just need

How long do I have

VITRUVIAN BOY

I used to lie
on the bathroom floor,

slip the smooth side
of a toothbrush into my hole.

I needed to know. I needed
to lie on the floor

for it to work.
When I was done, when I'd get up,

I couldn't wash away
my body's chalk

outline. Each one added to the others,
layered, multi-limbed,

a Leonardo sketch
of boyhood conscience.

It moved like stop-motion,
flip-book cartoon

convulsing,
swaying arms & legs.

I did it so much it became
a filled-in circle,

a white moon I knew one day
I'd have to lift like a city manhole.

All that silence
trapped underneath.

The tunnels
I'd have to go through,

return to,
concrete twists & turns

like the stomach
of an unknown god.

PORTRAIT OF A PARTIALLY ABANDONED CAMPGROUND

He's marrying a woman.

He who slipped down
his swim trunks in the pool,
wanted me to see the beautiful

serpent, wanted me
to risk my breath
beneath the surface.

I envied his boldness.

I craved his hand
that flitted to my branch
without notice.

I only came to life
around him, stringless
puppet.

The air he breathed had no
fear in it,
or at least, to me, he never showed it.

Mulch, night-grass,
bead of sweat between his legs,

the string of drip from his tip,

my lips, the vows we kept,
forgot, our separate tracks,
those woods, those trees, those stars overhead.

From the clearing
I look back,
small stack of smoke rising

from the dense.

II

We re uilty only o w ntin lowers.

We are guilty only of wanting flowers.

We are guilty only of wanting flowers.

We are guilty only of wanting flowers.

We are guilty only of wanting flowers.

We **a**re **g**uilty only o**f** w**a**ntin**g** **f**lowers.

VISITATION

For most of my life I was a liar, yes,
because I had to be, but I,
for most of my life, was still
a liar, lied even
to myself. For a while, I hated me.
Back then I hated
the secret me, hated me
secretly,
only to now look back & hate the me
that lied to me, to others.
Which me counts
as memory? Which lie was the I? The eye
watching me.
When I was finally ready, I woke
in my bed. A giant hummingbird
floated above me, long lancelike beak
piercing my body. It drank
from the red nectar of my chest.
Its long, forked tongue—yes two,
yes one.
It did not take my hate, but placed
a seed.

LEATHER BARS

I say, I'm gay but not
that gay.

The straight
laughs. I laugh

though my face
inside stays

straight. Facing it
straight on

is a room
with no

walls. The joke
hanging

in the air
between us

is the length
of a sword.

Only one end
is sharp.

AMY

My whole life I've had a gay aunt
& never knew it.

So obvious—went to Smith, no kids,
joked to us: "I forgot to get married!"

There was the lore of boyfriend Doug
from so long ago yet always brought up.

When I came out,
she called.

Her voice was full
of wingless doves

as she said, *I sort of*
had a feeling, at least, it's what I hoped.

Even in our liberal, lefty family
we spent my whole life staring at each other

through a two-way mirror.
I could only see myself.

She saw me, but could say nothing,
only watch.

Such a thin pane
between us.

Such thin pain, though clear now,
still keeps us.

I should call, I say.
Why don't I call?

To be gay is to wait,
to go airless,

to sit atop the moon
beside the ladder back down, back home,

to think: There's still so much I'd like to say
tomorrow.

F A G

Coworker Jim, irst out homosexu l I knew.

Down low I seduced him, still closeted, invitin mysel over.

His house w s my experiment, me discoverin com ort.

He s nk into love. I rew e rless enou h to un- ence,

voy e out. I le t him st ndin on the shore, l wless shell.

Who decides ri ht or cruel? or ye rs, I tried to pin

 uilt to my ormer sh dows. They moved throu h it,

 leshless. I m sorry I hurt you.

A WATER CYCLE

I followed him—the man wandering the woods, collecting
the fallen rain. Each drop a clear pearl he picked up,
then gently stashed in a blue satchel. From a distance, crouched
in the bushes, I studied his hands, his glittering fingers. I tried
to copy all his movements, but it never worked. I couldn't
grasp them, couldn't stop the drops from smashing
into tiny, ungrabbable lakes. My hands
weren't ready, hadn't learned yet the tender
language. I wanted to be like him, I wanted to like him, be
with him, but I didn't know it. Now, I know it. Now,
I wander the woods in my bright purple raincoat, my own
pearl necklace, doing the work. The damp air bears
witness, the rustling leaves, the quiet eyes hiding
within them.

CELEBRITY

I.

My aunt gifts me a book.

A memoir

about a gay man's funny life

being single.

I came out three years ago.

My aunt is harmless.

I add it to the pile with the others.

II.

Black sheep. Pink sheep. Green. Blue. Yellow. Rainbow
sheep.

I herd them beneath the great blanket of night.

I heard them.

III.

At a wedding in North Dakota,
we are the only gays. We are
celebrities. People shake our hands & say
how brave we are. On the dance floor,
we feel their gaze as they hang
on the edges of their seats. Will we
touch hands or, perhaps, lock lips?

IV.

In sixth grade, I used to say "that's gay" over & over.
Held up those words like a silver mirror
behind which I'd

cower.

V.

I wrote a poem about two ducks I saw walking off
into the sunset, so close I imagined little hands

being held beneath their feathers.
The first draft

I wrote *one male,*
one female.

VI.

"So who's the bride & who's the groom?"

(Who's fucking whom?)

Ask the willow tree
outside our window. Though I know
it'll never tell.

VII.

There I go again. ████ Self-
censorship. This ███ black bar
I hide ████████ my eyes
behind, ███ sometimes my
mouth, sometimes, yes, I
slip it ███████ inside myself.

VIII.

"Did you always know?"

(How many times have you lied to me?)

Here's a metaphor:

Someone skips a stone
across a lake. The stone skips on & on.
The stone is gay. The water of the lake is
truth.

IX.

You don't know me. I

don't know me,

but I'm

starting to.

X.

The book my aunt gave me: I   liked it.

I   read it twice,

I   bought a copy   for my

boyfriend.

AFTER SEEING QUEER TEENS HOLDING HANDS ON THE SIDEWALK

I remember he tried to kiss me,
so I blew him.

Cold cover of snowbank.

Memory, like landscapes, can be
transformed

with the right conditions.

That robin, wing-crushed,
on our path back from sledding—

I always saw as lips,
fragile thing that could have been,

what I wrecked.

Now, I see it's shapeless,
spilled blood,

a thrashing, red feeling,
anger—

not with myself,
not the blameless boy,

but that forest, snow-covered, stark
& unforgiving hour

that stretched across the afternoon,
the years—

knee-deep, but blank
as bone.

WITCHES

The boys with beards & heels
in the woods, in their circle, feral
for each other, for the night.
I am the owl in the tree,
eyes wide with shock—
& something else. Each boy
has no shadow, in the firelight, dancing
untethered. What spell draws me
closer, draws me out
from my barren hollow?
Turns my feathers into goose-bumped
skin—sweat-slick—am I dancing now
too? The air has no sound
but there is music. I am beautifully
flightless. Our heels grinding
into cold earth.

AT THE PROTEST, I LIST THE CONSEQUENCES OF COMING OUT

with a line by Federico García Lorca (tr. Catherine Brown)

1. I get to watch gay porn whenever I like.
2. When I'm done watching gay porn, I don't burn myself at the stake.
3. A voice, in the light, blooms.
4. I am no longer afraid of doors, of rooms.
5. Disapproving eyes, I wear like pearls.
6. Lots & lots of candy-colored nail polish.
7. Guilt only visits me a normal amount.
8. The word normal, now sour in the mouth.
9. Real Housewives.
10. RuPaul.
11. I get to use my real eyes, the ones I kept beneath the floorboards.
12. My mother knows me.
13. My father said out loud he loves me.
14. My brothers defend me.
15. Bobbleheads in robes want to tame me.
16. They cannot take away
17. Light.
18. Hands.
19. Our breath,
20. electric, between us.
21. It's too late.
22. *A thousand butterfly skeletons sleep within my walls.*
23. I am awake.

HE CAME TO ME AGAIN LAST NIGHT

Is my mind, this dream,
the only place he allows himself
to un-hide? To be free? We snuck out
from the cabin where our families
were sleeping to lie
in the snow. The trees all dressed
like brides. We snuck out like we did
when we were teens, risked ungloved hands
to feel skin. This time, I didn't feel
ashamed. I even went to kiss, but heard,
from close by, the low growl of muscled night,
the bear that followed him in.
He wanted us to run, so we did.
We barely made it. Inside,
in the cabin light, the snowflakes
dusting his eyes melted into tears.
I reached my hand to brush back
his hair. He flinched. I said,
I am so sorry. You can't come back.

THIS HALLOWEEN

Painted whiskers, black leather
choke collar, a little gold bell.
You've never looked
gayer, you say, & I'm in love—
with you, the orange
& the black, the sweet & the scary,
myself.
I'm on my second life, I say. The other seven—
a hoax, not guaranteed. I don't
need them.
This second skin I'm in,
I dig it. I
shimmer in it. I pounce & slink & don't feel like prey
for once.
I'm a kitty boy, pretty boy, boy who likes boys, boy
who tongues boy—ferocious,
playful, lazy in languor, a dream
I caught
with my claw.

HEATWAVE

There's nothing to do but
sit in stillness, root
for the lone window unit
huffing & puffing
cold smoke, though
useless. We do
what we must: peel off
our clothes,
first out of pure
necessity, but then
as we free our old
animal bodies,
it becomes something
different:

salt lick,
slick,

beautiful sweat
like diamonds

shimmering. O
we are shimmering.

Our hands,
four

magnificent
frigatebirds,

take turns

skimming

our surfaces.

We

forgot this.

TINY PANTS

At dinner, my mother tells you how, as an infant,
I used to call shorts *tiny pants.*

How, to this day, she & all my aunts
still use it as an adjective:

It was a *tiny pants* apartment,

a *tiny pants* plane cramped
& sweaty,

the party compared to last year was
tiny pants.

Our inside joke,
a little language of our own

& now you're part of it.

Before I proposed, I told my parents,

This is it.

This is the all-encompassing.
This is the floor-length, *big pants* love

I've been hoping for,

the two-legged truth:

continuation of tradition,

the start of something new.

III

When we uck, we spe k completely; ive to the other, the next line o the story.

When we fuck, we speak completely; give to the other, the next line of the story.

When we fuck, we speak completely; give to the other, the next line of the story.

When we fuck, we speak completely; give to the other, the next line of the story.

When we fuck, we speak completely; give to the other, the next line of the story.

When we **f**uck, we spe**a**k completely; **g**ive to the other, the next line o**f** the story.

THE NEWS THAT FELL LIKE HEAVY RAIN

for Natalie

B walks into the living room this next morning
& the first thing he says to me is
How's your heart?

I always struggle to know what I can't see.

You & I never actually met
though we talked on the phone once a week,

three years strong, watched volunteer work blossom
into bond.

I listened to you cry. We talked about your granddaughter
& God.

So nervous before our first call—gay boy from LA, you a pastor's wife
turned widow, turned pastor all yourself.

Survivor of hurricanes & Southern heat. The way, one year in,
you told me all about your own secret queer relationships.

People are impossible to fully know.

Starry sky we try to trap
in a thimble.

Your huge, celestial laughter.

How clovers grew in the cracks
of your voice.

A tunnel of flowers.

All I could see in my dream
was a tunnel of flowers,

the paper-cup phone, the long, taut string
cut.

MAN MARRIES MAN

Hard to believe in two months we'll be married. Tying
the knot, they say, though I think it's more of a great
untangling. Balled-up, twisted clump of string we carry
in our bodies. Your hands reaching into me, mine
into you. Slow, gentle, each undone knot a small sigh
of relief. Beneath the cold October sky, beneath birdsong,
red leaves lit by Maine sun, in front of all the ones we
love, we'll reach the final knots. & when the breeze blows
with the hum of our vows, the strings that kept both
our hidden selves bound will fall beside our feet. There,
we'll stand. There, we'll be.

WHEN THE WORLD ENDS, WE TAKE TURNS PLAYING DRESS-UP

In our front yard, I sit

beneath the willow.

Thin leaves cast

a pool of shadow, lace-like, that

in the wind, shifts & shimmers.

Pink snow, no—

little flowers. I almost cry

it's so peaceful, cool & quiet,

but then I notice

the metal zipper at the trunk's

base, the branches swaying though

windless. A cough.

I jump. Pull the zipper up

to find my husband

holding rods. Before I can ask

what happened to our willow,

I remember I am in

the future. Trees, here,

are endangered. Everyone's

an actor, desperate & nostalgic

for how it was.

AS THE CITY BURNED

Los Angeles, CA

Some of us ran, never to return.

Some of us watched. Some of us worked our same old jobs.

Some of us shopped, & some of us went

  for a walk or a jog without wearing a mask.

Some of us answered the worried texts.

Some of us stopped. Some of us couldn't stop

  putting ourselves at the center of it all.

Some of us who weren't even there wanted it

  political.

Some of us helped. Some hugged. Some even said hello to a stranger

  in a checkout line, who then said it back.

Some of us died.

Some of us lost everything but our lives.

Some of us lost nothing at all, except maybe

  hope in the future, in the way things are.

Some of us dream of the day the term "all of us"

  will finally be used in a serious way.

All of us are afraid.

All of us   want change,

  want to stop the flames

  from being meaningless.

STILL, DAYS

While I ate my oatmeal, I saw Hope on the milk carton.
What's missing: hope, the milk carton.

I tried to write hope into a poem, but couldn't.

The words scattered like iron filings anytime my hands
came near them. Everything has its own magnetic field of sadness.

A friend told me there are mountains in Upstate New York
with no fossils, formed before life.

What feels impossible: time, to be stone-clean, to be
unmovable.

Today's losses were the heaviest they've ever been.

I tried to punch pain's ticket, make it leave on
clear tracks down my cheeks, but it wouldn't.

Still, days. Still days. I am full of pain & fossils.

I think I gave up a few lines ago, the poem on grief,
or was it hope?

I turn off the lights. The poem glows.

WHAT YOU FORGOT

Why are you crying? he says.

The tree, I say. It's dying.

Which tree? he says.

The one I grow from, I say.

Humans don't grow on trees, he says.

Yes, I say. They do.

I grab his hand & pull it

to the invisible branch

sprouting from my back.

Do you feel it? I say.

His eyes, wide, hands cupping air—

Yes, he says. I do.

You have one too, I say,

pointing to his back.

He becomes very quiet.

& here, I say,

my hand at his chest,

fruit.

THE GARDEN STATE

Here, people live green days,
wake to hundreds of softly colored
birds.
In the woods, children lose then find
            themselves.
Fathers tend their gardens
even after all their sons
            have left them.

It's been three years since you've visited
in June.
            You've forgotten
what lush is, the sight
            of roots.

Back in your desert, the only green things
            are dreams—spiked & dry.

In this breeze, you see
how tall the trees are, taller
than you remember, & you like
once again feeling
            small,

feeling a wall of leaves curl
around you.

You plant a question in the ground
beside your father's
            strawberries.

You leave
before it blooms.

ON THE PHONE

for C

I think I miss the goats, you tell me,
the herd your town brought in
to mow unruly pastures.
At the end of your road, for two whole weeks,
you'd visit them, while they roamed & ate
& watched you with their strange yellow eyes
you wished were real-life mail slots
for sending your loneliest letters.
I wish I could bend myself into a paper
swan, takeout menu, napkin with a
grandma's scarlet lipstick on the rim
& surprise you. A long, but only 64-cent
voyage. Then you could unfold me
like a paper fortune-teller
& every one of my insides would read:
I'm sorry I'm not a goat, but I love you.
I miss them too, I say, having never met them.
& sometimes it feels like our friendship
lives outside of us, a mycelium,
all of our laughter & stories & memories
& nonsense threaded together.
We can't always see it, but it's as real as the ground
we walk on, as the trees that whisper silly
things & the best part is knowing
we both can hear them.

RAIN ON THE FOURTH

Brainerd, MN

I stood beneath the sliver of roof
at the front door. You & your mother
sat side by side on the stoop.
You closed your eyes. The invisible
left its mark all over your shirts.
Unmistakable smell of summer
road, childhood home. I walked my bare
feet on the lawn & hundreds of baby toads
leaped. A good plague. A tiny firework.
Your dad asleep inside post-
chemo. His first week. Thunder,
then harder rain. Eventually
we went inside to play games,
eat the ice cream your sister made.
On the long flight home,
you & I saw, below, a cloud beating
with light. Someone else's storm.
How easily we passed above it. How strange
it felt.

CLOSER

I'm thinking about his cock
when I look up

& see two huge chemtrails
crossed, a cloud crucifix.

Years ago, in the closet, I would
have yelped, thought

            There goes, again,
Jesus in the fighter jet.

            Stop thinking about hard
men.
                                    Repent, Repent.

When straight people write about sex
it's love.

When gay people write about sex it's
too much.

            What if Uncle Sam reads it?

            What if Aunt Sally swallows
a lung?

What if thc kids, the kids
believe it? See

an antidote
to silence, to

Don't Say . . . what?

Our normal. Our new
religion—

His tongue.   My bum-
rush. The way I arch my back

when I come
undone, undone.

F A G

Do I count i I've never spoken   wish
into the lory hole? I I've never worn
le ther? Never lost my own body's silk
in the pile twistin tree roots so ine, so
deliber tely slow they don't seem
to be movin . To eel the che, relentless
ton ues o sh red ni ht. The l kes,
  old,   llin   rom where? Whom? I h ve
one love, yes, us two, to ether
  orever, but this third sh dow is whose?

ON THE EVE OF OUR WEDDING

I walked the green field & the world stopped turning, slowed
like a playground carousel.

I felt still ground with my feet, thought
we'd be sucked into space,

or worse, left to wait—eternal day for some,
others, the death of light.

When I woke, I wanted to know
why, spent all morning teasing out every detail—

Was it a sign? A bad omen
for our marriage? The end

of a life?

You called my name & I realized what my dream-god
was sharing:

Stop the huge, huge head from spinning,
spinning, always spinning.

Look up—
            see him.

A SUMMER CAMP WEDDING

Waterford, Maine, September 29th–October 2nd, 2022

My Mother, One Year Out

Are you sure? Won't it be cold? How will you feed everyone?
What happens if it rains? If it pours? If people don't come
because it's so, so far? Why not LA? Why not
a Hollywood-themed, Gatsby
of a night?

—

You, One Year Out

Trust me.

—

Costco

Four whole carts full of booze, marshmallows.
Your dad, in his scooter, waits 45 minutes
for a cherry icee.

The checkout guy asks us to place our bets
on the cost:

Everything.

Nothing.

—

En Route

The drive from Portland to Camp Waziyatah
is void of highways.

Just one long, uninterrupted road, through leaves, changing.

—

The Guests Arrive

Steady stream
of light.

—

First Night

New England cold sticks to us like blue glue.
In the morning, we are sleepless, but
laughing &
bonded.

—

At the Kickball Game

140 blue & green sweatshirts move
like a new, limbed sea. Once-separate strangers now
a single body:

Uncle Pat starts the team chant, "Drink Heavily!"

Naz skips second base, chortles uncontrollably.

The ball flies through the air & Aunt Katie
catches it. Aunt Katie flies through the air

weightless.

—

First Look

Down the cabin steps & there
you are, back turned, tall
in your green suit, perfect statue
framed by red leaves, glassy
water.

You hear my footsteps
& crack, small tremor
running through your body

before I even
tap.

—

Ceremony

All day: no wind, just sun & son & son.
The warmth of love, it hugs.

My dad & brother play the guitar. Len sings.
We walk.

—

Dog Days Are Over

comes on & the dance floor transports
to another plane.
We are freed of time & space. We are all here,
somewhere, witnessing.

—

When Everyone is Gone

Your parents sit in the packed car. One last time, we walk
the dock, watch
the yellow trees breathe. We cry
luminescent tears, release them
like minnows in the water.

—

My Mother, Two Days Later

It was like Woodstock! It was like we all saw
a UFO! It was

an experience, a feeling
we can't quite name.

—

Back Home

I search
for the weekend's
one loose thread,

to pull it back.

I find
your hand.

HIS FINGER WITH THE NINJA TURTLES BAND-AID

Late sunlight pooling
on the hardwood.

You walk by & pick it up
like dropped laundry.

Gold, shimmering sheet.

You fold it, then gently
place it in the cupboard.

For later,
you turn to me.

IV

riend—we le ve the window open, world peekin in.

Friend—we leave the window open, world peeking in.

Friend—we leave the window open, world peeking in.

Friend—we leave the window open, world peeking in.

Friend—we leave the window open, world peeking in.

Friend—we le**a**ve the window open, world peekin**g** in.

FIRST TIME WE'VE SEEN HER SINCE THE WEDDING

Right now, your mother's soaring
over Salt Lake City, will be here
till Tuesday.

We'll carve the ugly pumpkin,
show her green thumb
the Huntington Gardens.

She & I will be up
early, while you snooze.

She'll make, from her travel coffee kit,
a couple strong pour-overs.

I'll read her my newest poems.
She'll cry.

I'll call her *Mom*.

TOO MANY LOOSE SHOES IN THE CLOSET

When I said the words "I'm gay," my father
shut like an oyster. My mother was sunny, then
pouring, ironically already wearing
her raincoat. In the morning, my mother
went missing. My father made me manic pancakes,
watched me eat them. Eggs for eyes,
bacon smile. Every sentence spoken was a train
with no cargo, headed to tomorrow,
& the next day. We swept, or better yet,
all together pulled, the giant vintage rug
over our heads. Now, we're happy, really.
We get along. They love my hub, understand
my life in LA, why it was necessary.
But in my deepest sleep, my father's teeth
are round, glistering. There
for the taking. A string of wealth.
If I risk my hand. If I reach in,
reach out.

OUR FIRST TURKEY

cooked upside down for two hours
before the thought *Where are the legs?*
finally won & I took it out & you
palmed the 21-pound bird
with dirty oven mitts.
& didn't both of us, at some point, feel
face down & drowning? Years of thinking
something's wrong with us? Look—unfolding
in the dining room: our longest table,
mostly women, gays,
a Last Supper scene that would
have gagged even the wisest men.
Wine swirling our faces pink. The laughter
spreading seat to seat
breaks us, breaks down
our fixed ideas. Turns out—
the turkey's great.
Maggie says it's the juiciest she's ever had
& she's a turkey freak.
We *Cheers!* Eat pie. Play a murder mystery
& when the last friend leaves,
you & I, we fall asleep
in our big blue bed, our naked chests open
to the sky.

DINNER PARTY

I stuff the dishwasher.

You, in the dining room, sweep up the crumbs
        of laughter.

A little wine-drunk. The house still aglow.

People will remember us
        for nights like this, you say.

& I feel a shift inside my chest—

        a tunnel,
                opening.

F A G

riendly older wom n eyes my reen crewneck,

the estive summer c mp lo o, smiles, then tries to pry us

rom the tense USPS quiet, sks ently, i I went there.

I expl in our weddin . She smirks, *un one, ren't you! osh,*

your wi e is lucky. I ddress nothin .

I orm my mouth into vow to silence— ive it li e, blood, bre th. I,

its mistress.

I HEAR THE SHOWER SHUTTING OFF

after D.A. Powell

Jotting down my last thought
before this world ends,
by which I mean
before you come in here completely
naked.

My angel, fallen,
keep searching for those lost wings
inside me.
I hope
you never find them.

Each time you come
the world ends,
by which I mean
begins.
A sudden bursting.

REFLEX

Not once growing up did I realize
the insult *You suck*

must have been a shortened version of
You suck cock

because what is more damning,
more demeaning than

a gay boy dreaming
of a hard-on?

Fem men, receiving,
men on their knees,

throats open, singing
the wet & sloppy song.

My god, when it's thick
& long—I impress

even myself, my gag
reflex. Where's the Nobel Prize

for shortest time
to make him cum?

Call it wrong,
but know you'd be screaming right

if you had my eyes
at your hips,

if you were lucky enough
to catch a glimpse

of me
working it—your stick, twin stones,

my own
breathless words

pumping up
into your veins,

chest, the edge
of your lips—

Yes, yes, yes.

FAG

in lly posted the poem on bottomin .

TikTok erupted with comments.

Vile little letters, but not rom str i ht men.

irst: *This poem sucks.* Then:

This is why blue st tes turn red, why we lose

our ri hts. s don't see their own ury,

sh rp seed dropped inside the belly.

The rowth is whose ult? We do

the uilty work o someone else.

THE HOMOSEXUAL AGENDA

1.

A twink walks into the Republican National Convention

& opens Grindr, causing:

a big, gay, red wave,

the app to crash.

No wonder they're obsessed

with body politics.

It's a shame

about shame.

2.

In 2016, my father voted for him.
In 2020, I pleaded in an email, saying:

Hello, Dad. I am your son.

Linked the article where he joked
about Pence, "Don't ask that guy—
he wants to hang them all!"

Good to hear from you, my father replied,
This is important to know.

If my mother was telling me the truth,
my father
didn't vote.

3.

Today, I get an email from a sperm bank saying, *Want to make $15k??*
Saying, *We understand you're gay & will finally be able to donate.*

Only a year ago, the FDA lifted its restrictions on gay & bi men
donating to blood banks.

It stings a little. How quickly they act like nothing was wrong,
like their laws didn't say to us: *You may exist*

so long as everything about you stays
within your skin.

4.

My husband & I host our British friend, Amy, for a few weeks.
We eat chicken breast then laugh at *Veep*, explain to her
what the filibuster is so she gets the joke. Between episodes,
Brian says we should go to Transylvania, shows us a beautiful
castle, quiet trees. I google *Can gay people travel to Romania?*
& find out homosexuality was decriminalized in 2002,
that no laws exist there against homosexuals, except marriage.
After a silence, Amy says, *It's so completely wild*
you have to ask that.

5.

Can gay people travel to Jamaica?
Can gay people travel to Hungary?
Can gay people travel to Qatar?
Can gay people travel to Bali?
What about Egypt?
What about Missouri?
Where is it safe?
Where is it safe
to be?

6.

There's something so gay about the moon.
So glittery & up-all-night-thinking.

Mike says every gay man has a pop-
girlie-diva they worship.

I've decided: She is mine.
Femme. All-American. Girl next door

in the sky. Crowned Queen
Unafraid of Night, unafraid

to belt a silent song,
to give every sleepless

little boy a slice, a real reason
to shine.

7.

The election is just around the corner.

I don't think my father will vote for him

but there is a nagging thought, countdown clock.

An email burrows in my drafts:

Dear Dad,

Dear Dad,

What am I

if not

your own

thrashing

blood?

8.

Unfortunately for you:

The cat's out of the bag. One flew over the cuckoo's nest & never came back.

Pandora's box. Life is like a heart of chocolates I buy for my husband at CVS.

You never know what you're going to get, except you do: Win or lose,

we keep coming back. Bootstraps. Leather harness, assless, not less ass. We are

defiance. We are like moonlight, iridescent, inescapable in night. We are

moonshine drunk on our rights our rights our rights.

COPYRIGHT

On the phone, my mom asks me
how I am. I say, *Good*, without telling her
about my upcoming reading,
where I'll recite the poem
about Dad's politics, my
shame. Sometimes being out
is another form of hiding.
A single kite in the sky
three sets of hands
are flying.
I want to tell my mom *I'm sorry*.
I want to tell my mom: The kite
is not a kite, but a bird
we tied to string.
Am I right? To take the blade
& cut it free?
To leave each hand
exposed,
empty?

AIRBNB

A little drunk, laughing at a joke—
though all still a bit on edge
being in a strange house
in the middle of the woods—

we go around the dinner table & say
the first time we remember
feeling proud.
An odd question, something

no one ever asks, which is either
an indictment of us, or society,
or both.
It's easy to talk about pain,

feeling lost, the special ways
in which our parents
fucked us up.
But Angel tells us

the time he wrote an essay in sixth grade
his teacher read aloud.
& as he recounts the story
I watch the blossoms

in his face, something forgotten
floating up to the surface, & I realize—

in this moment, because of it,
I *know* him.

& the circle continues, as does
the laughter, the mushrooms
we take to go even deeper.
& the moon softly streams through

the window, as if by faucet,
& we are grateful.
& although no one says it, out of fear
of being cheesy, we all can feel it—

this fixture, signpost on the road years from now
the four of us, whether still together
or on our separate paths,
can point to. A map. The night's pins of light. Receipt that proves

we lived our lives.

RAIN

Today it rains. Here, where it never
rains, so I go walk in it,
umbrellaless, & feel the wet
pinpricks on my cheeks, my nose,
my eyelids. Each small drop,
a clear thought of aliveness
that wakes my body up.
This body I take for granted.
This body I throw cruel words
at. This body that drinks in rain,
then sends thin rivers of shivers
down the spine.
This body I will one day
leave behind. Late at night,
awake & shapeless in the purple sky,
I will cry out for it.

AT THE END OF ANOTHER SAD GAY MOVIE

There were tears, but invisible. & mirrors. Looking
into mirrors, then looking away. There were holes
in logic, in truth, old moth-bitten sweaters, holes I dug,
called home. Not many calls home, but there was smoke,
but really, fog. Yes, there was a fog machine I
controlled & no one else. There were alleys, back seats,
black eyes, bloody nose. The slow transforming
into ghost[1]

---

[1]then

A gathering, inside the body, birds blue red orange
migrating. There were words, many. Faces, small & blank
as seeds, later grew into smiles. There was laughter.
A meet-cute. Green olives swimming in dry martinis.
A house. A cat. A marriage. The dream
of a garden. There were days we did absolutely nothing.
Couches, body pillows, burgers delivered.
There were days we opened the closet to only five strips
of darkness. Limbs tied to the bed. Blindfolded. Lips.
Skin erupted in goosebumps. There was light. So much light,
we carried it. He & I. We handed it out to all who passed by,
armfuls, life's lemons iridescent rolling to the ground
like ellipses. We were walking. We're still
walking, off into the sunset, no, sunrise. It's only
morning.

FROM THE WINDOW

You, with the cat, out back
like brothers in summer

slipping through grass,
watching chickadees perform their number

in the branch's theater—rapt,
untouchable except by cool wind,

shadows cast
by thin bamboo. I love

the two of you, the pureness,
backyard silence, the day's smooth

undisturbed surface. Even
impermanence,

even twilight's slow undoing
of all of this.

The pang. The stone
inside the fruit. Again, again

I choose it.

AFTER READING MY NEW MANUSCRIPT

C tells me, *The book needs*
conflict. It's one big exhale
without an inhale, if that makes sense.
& it does. & I reply, *Doesn't everyone want*
to feel relief? "Times
like these." & they do. But every note
has its unexplored core—small, silver pool reflecting
life. Isn't having no conflict
a good thing? The always staying in. No bars,
no restaurants. The decade-long "temporary" day job. This
quiet marriage,
so unlike our other gay friends who run their bodies wild
through the field of poppies. My god—
I've never tried poppers! Or had a threesome.
Or found God in a K-hole on a sticky, sweaty dance floor.
Both my parents are still living. All my siblings
are healthy & beautiful & so
are their children. Can't afford children—that's conflict.
Feel inadequate in every room I enter—also conflict.
Scared to make small talk with my upstairs neighbor
so I hide while taking out the garbage.
Last night though, I watched him carry his newborn
through the dusky backyard—pointing out
the hummingbird feeder, the bamboo, then
proudly lowering her chubby face to the planter boxes
so her barely usable eyes could see
the shoots of lettuce,

cherry tomatoes on the vine still green, still free
of conflict. Her whole life ahead of her, this small body just
the first syllable. *I guess it's inevitable,* I tell C, conflict
always just around the corner.
& maybe, when it comes, those poems I write
will pop off the page, or make C cry, or maybe
they'll drip with a deep-seated regret for all
I've never tried—& that's okay.
& maybe I'll wait. Or maybe I'll try just
a little harder, & lift my head,
wave
at the father & daughter passing by.

THE FUTURE

We're standing on a hilltop.

From here, if you squint your eyes, you can just
see it, he says.

Is it small because of distance? I ask,
or because—decay—so much of it already
fallen away?

I'm not sure, he says.

I stare at the sky & a long, gray cloud
fills me.

Quick, he says, *lie down.*

So I do.

He takes off my shoes
& with
a gentle push—I roll

slow, at first,
then faster, then laughter
tumbles out like

paper birds.

FOR IF I GO FIRST

My sweet man, tall man, bub, love
of my life:
                I am *here*.
                                Whether or not heaven
exists, these lines
                        are real.

        I am here in these lines speaking to you, outside
        time,
space. This page,
                where I wait for you, for your visits. When you need a break
from your life that's kept on moving, the jobs, more love, more loss.

        I am here. Tell me about them.
                Come pitch a tent. We can make stars, as many
                as we want.
                We can travel back to that first & only camping trip.

We can make nothing. We can leave this page but a satin sheet
        to lie on. The thin veil is nothing more than your mother's quilt,
        the one she made me—blue-green
                like a shallow sea.

        My husband, my one & only, weren't we so lucky?

        To have found each other. That everything between us came
        clear.

                Utopia,
                        here, *here*.

What we have will never end. I've penned it
    that way. Carved out this space—for us.

I am here.
I am here.
I love you.
Oh god, how I love you.

DARK SUNDAY

We stay in bed all day.

The pen stands up & writes the poem
without me.

Your fingers graze my back.

I pull your body over me
like a roof, mistake

your drumming heart
for rain.

NOTES

"At the Protest, I List the Consequences of Coming Out" (p. 38): The line "*A thousand butterfly skeletons sleep within my walls*" is borrowed from Federico García Lorca's poem "Hour of Stars" translated by Catherine Brown, published in the revised edition of *The Collected Poems: A Bilingual Edition* (Farrar, Straus and Giroux, 2002).

"As the City Burned" (p. 51): This poem was written after the Palisades and Eaton Wildfires, which in early January 2025 destroyed 37,469 acres of land in Los Angeles County (CBS News).

"Closer" (p. 58): The line "*Don't say* . . . what?" is a reference to Florida's Don't Say Gay bill passed in March 2022.

"A Summer Camp Wedding" (p. 62): The song mentioned, "Dog Days Are Over," is by Florence + the Machine.

"I Hear the Shower Shutting Off" (p. 76): This poem drew inspiration from D.A. Powell's poem "Tarnished Angel," published in the collection *Useless Landscape, or A Guide for Boys* (Graywolf Press, 2012).

"The Homosexual Agenda" (p. 80): This poem was originally written for the event Poetry *is* Democracy, hosted by the MFA Creative Writing Program at Antioch University Los Angeles.

— Section 1 (p. 80) was written as a cheeky response to the unconfirmed (but viral) reports of the gay dating app, Grindr, crashing several times during the 2024 Republican National Convention in Milwaukee.

— Section 2 (p. 80) references a quote originally published in a 2017 article of *The New Yorker*, titled "The Danger of President Pence," by Jane Mayer.

— Section 3 (p. 81) references an FDA ruling in May 2023 allowing gay and bisexual men in monogamous relationships to donate blood without abstaining from sex.

— Sections 4 and 5 (p. 81 & 82) got their information from the websites Human Dignity Trust and ACLU.

— In Section 8 (p. 83) the lines "Life is like a heart of chocolates I buy for my husband at CVS. / You never know what you're going to get, except you do . . ." is a play on the very famous quote from the 1994 film *Forrest Gump*: "My mama always said life was like a box of chocolates. You never know what you're gonna get."

ACKNOWLEDGMENTS

Thank you to the following journals where some of these poems first appeared, sometimes in previous forms:

& Change—"I Hear the Shower Shutting Off," "Dinner Party"
ALOCASIA—"Cruising"
Atlanta Review—"The Prayers of Mice"
Bear Review—"Dark Sunday"
Birdcoat Quarterly—"Witches"
DIALOGIST—"Vitruvian Boy"
Gulf Stream—"Little Quaint House"
Hayden's Ferry Review—"Portrait of a Partially Abandoned Campground"
Hole in the Head Review—"After Seeing Queer Teens Holding Hands on the Sidewalk," "Our First Turkey"
JanusWords—"The Poker Game"
Juke Joint—"Still, Days," "The Beginning of Love"
Kitchen Table Quarterly—"At the End of Another Sad Gay Movie"
Laurel Review—"Too Many Loose Shoes in the Closet"
Palette Poetry—"f a g [Do I count . . .]"
Passengers Journal—"He Came to Me Again Last Night"
River Heron Review—"What You Forgot"
Saranac Review—"A Water Cycle," "Heatwave," "When the World Ends, We Take Turns Playing Dress-up"
Solstice: A Magazine of Diverse Voices—"Gay Voice"
Sprung Formal—"f a g [Coworker Jim, rst . . .]," "f a g [irst pet ls in . . .]," "f a g [Ben, best riend . . .]"
The Florida Review—"On the Phone," "Rain on the Fourth"
The Los Angeles Review—"Amy"
Tiny Spoon—"At the Protest, I List the Consequences of Coming Out"
Tupelo Quarterly—"Celebrity"
Two Hawks Quarterly—"The News That Fell like Heavy Rain"
West Trade Review—"Leather Bars"